MAKE
MIXES
FOR FAST FIXES
MW01616784

How to use this book

Begin by stirring up one or more dry master mixes ahead of time, then store each in an airtight container in your cupboard or fridge. When you're craving homemade baked goodies, just choose a recipe and combine a few cups of your master mix with the recipe's fresh ingredients and yummy extras – so simple and so delicious!

For best results, stir master mixes before using, and use large eggs and room temperature ingredients. The icons on each recipe indicate the correct oven temperature and approximate baking time.

ISBN-13: 978-1-56383-533-9
Item #7140

**Printed in the USA
by G&R Publishing Co.**

Distributed By:

507 Industrial Street
Waverly, IA 50677

www.cqbookstore.com

gifts@cqbookstore.com

 CQ Products

 CQ Products

 @cqproducts

 @cqproducts

Check out these other tips for perfect baked products every time.

Muffins

- **Pan prep:** Grease muffin cups with shortening or cooking spray or use paper liners *(spritz them with cooking spray for extra-easy removal).*

- Muffin batters should be lumpy, not smooth, so avoid over-mixing.

- Fill muffin cups ⅔ to ¾ full and bake promptly. *(An ice cream scoop makes this simple and neat.)*

- When done, muffins should have rounded tops and be lightly browned. A toothpick inserted in the center should come out clean.

Quick Breads

- **Pan prep:** Brush shortening over the bottom and ½" up the sides of loaf pans.

- Don't over-mix quick bread batters – a few lumps are fine if batter is well combined.

- Fill loaf pans ⅔ full and bake right away. To prevent overbrowning, cover loaf with foil for the last 15 minutes of baking.

- Let quick bread cool in its pan for 10 minutes before removing to a wire rack to finish cooling.

- Cut when completely cool, or wrap cooled loaves in plastic wrap and cut the next day *(especially fruit breads).*

Cookies

- **Pan prep:** Line cookie sheets with parchment paper.

- Master mix cookie doughs are mixed differently and will be rather thick – try not to over-work.

- Use a pastry blender or two knives to cut shortening or softened butter into the master mix.

- Use an electric mixer to beat ingredients together when directed, but stop when the dough comes together or the mixer slows down. Beat in a spoonful of water as needed, and stir in extra ingredients with a sturdy spoon.

- For uniform drop cookies, use a cookie scoop to drop the dough.

- Prefer extra-crisp cookies? Bake them at 375° instead.

- Cool cookies on the pan about 5 minutes before transferring to a wire rack to cool completely.

Bars & Brownies

- **Pan prep:** Grease the bottom of pan or prep as directed in each recipe.

- Fudgy brownies are done when a toothpick inserted near the center comes out with a few moist crumbs clinging.

- Cut cooled brownies with a plastic knife.

- One 18.3 ounce package of purchased brownie mix contains about 3 cups, so measure accordingly if using your homemade mix for other favorite recipes needing a boxed mix.

Cakes & Cupcakes

- **Pan prep:** Grease and flour all cake and Bundt pans before using; use liners for cupcakes.

- Fill cupcake liners ½ to ⅔ full.

- Cakes test done when a toothpick inserted in the center comes out clean or when cake begins to pull away from edges of pan and springs back when the center is pressed lightly.

- To remove cake, let cool 10 minutes and then invert pan onto a serving platter, tapping bottom lightly to release cake.

- Cool cakes and cupcakes before frosting.

Biscuits & More

- **Pan prep:** Line cookie sheets with parchment paper or follow recipe instructions.

- Handle dough as little as possible to get tender biscuits and shortcakes.

- Don't over-mix batters.

Yeast Breads

- **Pan prep:** Line baking sheets with parchment paper or follow recipe instructions.

- Heat liquids in the microwave or on the stovetop, and test the temperature with a thermometer before adding to the master mix. *(If water is too cold, the yeast won't activate; if too hot, it kills the yeast.)*

- To help yeast breads rise well, place a pan of hot water on the bottom rack of a cold oven and set bread dough on the top rack; cover with a light towel. Turn on the oven light, too – it's the perfect combo of warmth and moisture to activate yeast.

- To flatten dough before shaping and pop any big air bubbles, use your hands or a rolling pin.

- If dough springs back when shaping, let it rest 5 minutes to help it relax, then continue.

- Shape dough so it is nice and smooth on top; pinch seams on the bottom side and place seam side down in the pan.

- Use a pizza cutter to slice dough for breadsticks and pretzels, etc.

- A sturdy stand mixer with a paddle beater is the best tool to mix yeast doughs – dough hooks are optional.

One batch of this master mix is enough to prepare six different muffin or quick bread recipes.

Muffin Master Mix

12½ C. all-purpose flour
5 T. baking powder
1 T. baking soda
2 tsp. salt

¾ C. light brown sugar *(packed)*
4 C. sugar

Combine all ingredients in a very large bowl and mix with a wire whisk or your hands to break up any lumps. Transfer to a labeled airtight container and store in a cool, dry place.

Before using, stir the mix to redistribute ingredients evenly, as settling may occur. Use as directed in the recipes that follow.

Shelf life 3-4 months

Fresh Apple Muffins

Mix 2 eggs, 1 C. milk, 1 C. peeled, grated apple, ½ C. melted butter, and 1 tsp. cinnamon. Stir in **2¾ C. Muffin Mix** until just combined. Spoon batter into prepped muffin cups and sprinkle with **Nutty Streusel** *(page 62)*. Bake as indicated or until muffins test done. *Makes 12-16 muffins*

 400°  15-18 min.

Orange Chocolate Chip Muffins

Whisk 2 eggs with ½ C. orange juice, ½ C. milk, ½ C. melted butter, and 2 tsp. orange zest. Stir in **2¾ C. Muffin Mix** until just blended; fold in 1½ C. chocolate chips. Spoon batter into prepped muffin cups and bake as indicated. While warm, drizzle with **Orange Glaze** *(page 61)*. *Makes 18 muffins*

 400°  15-18 min.

Sweet 'n' Cheesy Muffins

¼ C. vegetable oil
1 egg
1¼ C. buttermilk
½ tsp. white or black pepper
½ tsp. salt
¼ C. chopped fresh chives

½ C. shredded
cheddar cheese
¼ C. diced onion
¼ C. shredded
Parmesan cheese
2¾ C. Muffin Mix

Mix the first nine ingredients together, whisking well. Add **Muffin Mix** and stir until just combined. Spoon batter into prepped muffin cups and bake as indicated or until muffins test done. *Makes 12-16 muffins*

350°

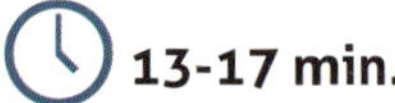
13-17 min.

Almond Poppy Seed Bread

½ C. vegetable oil
2 eggs
1 (6 oz.) carton lowfat
  vanilla yogurt
2 tsp. almond extract

¼ C. milk
1½ T. poppy seed
3 C. Muffin Mix
Sliced almonds

Mix the first six ingredients together, whisking well. Add **Muffin Mix** and stir until just combined. Spread batter in a prepped 5 x 9" loaf pan and sprinkle with almonds. Bake as indicated or until bread tests done. *Makes 1 loaf*

*For **Lemon Poppy Seed Bread**, substitute lemon yogurt and lemon extract, and add 1 T. lemon zest.*

 **350°** 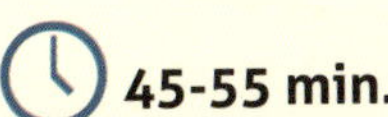 **45-55 min.**

9

Pumpkin Chip & Nut Bread

½ C. vegetable oil
2 eggs
1 C. milk
1 C. pumpkin puree
1 tsp. vanilla
1½ tsp. cinnamon

½ tsp. allspice
3 C. Muffin Mix
½ to ¾ C. semi-sweet
  chocolate chips
½ C. chopped pecans

Mix the first seven ingredients together, then add the **Muffin Mix** and stir until just combined. Fold in chocolate chips and pecans. Spread batter in a prepped 5 x 9" loaf pan and bake as indicated or until bread tests done. *Makes 1 loaf*

 350°

 55-65 min.

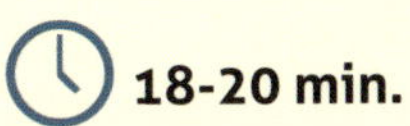

Salted Caramel Muffins

¼ C. butter, melted
1 C. buttermilk
1 egg
¼ C. canola oil
1 T. vanilla

¼ C. brown sugar
2½ C. Muffin Mix
Caramel topping
Coarse salt
Pecan pieces, optional

Whisk together the first six ingredients. Add **Muffin Mix** and stir until just combined. Spoon batter into prepped muffin cups and bake as indicated or until muffins test done. Just before serving, drizzle muffins with caramel topping, sprinkle with salt, and top with a few pecan pieces, if you'd like. *Makes 12-15 muffins*

11

Sweet Cornbread

Whisk ½ C. vegetable oil with 2 eggs and 1 C. milk; stir in 1 C. sweet corn *(fresh or frozen, thawed)*. Add **2¼ C. Muffin Mix** and 1 C. yellow cornmeal, stirring until just combined. Spread in a greased 8 x 8" baking pan and sprinkle with 2 T. coarse sugar. Bake as indicated or until bread tests done. *Makes 1 square pan*

 350°  35-45 min.

Pistachio Zucchini Bread

Mix ½ C. vegetable oil, 2 eggs, 1 C. buttermilk, ½ C. grated zucchini, ½ tsp. nutmeg, and 1 tsp. cinnamon. Stir in **3 C. Muffin Mix** until just combined. Fold in 1 C. chopped pistachios. Spread in a prepped loaf pan; sprinkle with **Cinnamon-Sugar** *(page 62)*. Bake as indicated or until bread tests done. *Makes 1 loaf*

 350° 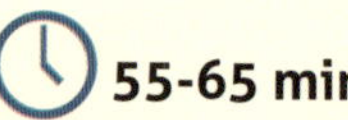 55-65 min.

Chocolate-Cherry Nut Bread

Mix 2 eggs, 1 C. milk, 1 tsp. vanilla, ½ C. melted butter, and ¾ C. unsweetened cocoa powder. Stir in **2½ C. Muffin Mix** until combined. Fold in ¾ C. chopped pecans, 1½ C. chopped maraschino cherries, and 1 C. chocolate chips *(optional)*. Spread in a prepped loaf pan and bake as indicated or until bread tests done. *Makes 1 loaf*

 350°  50-60 min.

Vanilla Chip Muffins

Stir together ½ C. melted butter, 2 eggs, 1 C. milk, and 1½ tsp. vanilla. Stir in **2¼ C. Muffin Mix** and 1 C. coarsely crushed corn flakes until just combined. Fold in 1 C. vanilla baking chips. Spoon batter into prepped muffin cups and bake as indicated or until muffins test done. Drizzle with melted chips *(optional)*.
Makes 12-16 muffins

 400° 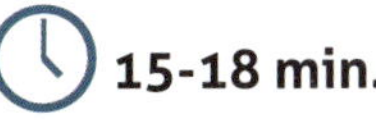 15-18 min.

13

Blueberry-Oatmeal Muffins

½ C. butter, melted

2 eggs

1 tsp. lemon extract

1 C. buttermilk

1 C. fresh berries *(we used blueberries)*

2 C. Muffin Mix

1 C. quick oats

Nutty Streusel *(recipe on page 62)*

Whisk the first four ingredients together and set aside. In another bowl, toss berries with **Muffin Mix** until coated; stir in set-aside buttermilk mixture and oats until just combined. Spoon batter into prepped muffin cups and sprinkle with some **Nutty Streusel**. Bake as indicated or until muffins test done.

Makes 18 muffins

 400° 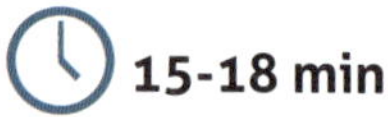 15-18 min.

Cranberry Burst Muffins

¾ C. plain or vanilla yogurt
⅓ C. canola oil
1 egg
1 tsp. vanilla
2 T. lemon juice
1 T. lemon zest

1½ C. fresh or frozen *(thawed)* cranberries, chopped
½ C. yellow cornmeal
2 C. Muffin Mix
Zested Sugar *(recipe on page 62)*

Whisk together the first six ingredients; set aside. In another bowl, toss cranberries with cornmeal until coated. Add the **Muffin Mix** and cranberry combo to the set-aside yogurt mixture, stirring until just combined. Spoon batter into prepped muffin cups and sprinkle with **Zested Sugar**. Bake as indicated or until muffins test done. *Makes 12-14 muffins*

 400° 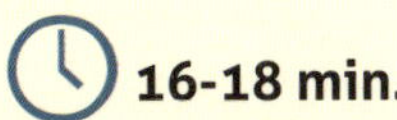 16-18 min.

15

Cookie Master Mix

9 C. all-purpose flour
1 T. baking soda
2 tsp. baking powder
2 tsp. salt

3 C. sugar
2¼ C. light brown sugar
   (packed)

Combine all ingredients in a very large bowl and whisk well, using your hands to break up any lumps. Transfer to a labeled airtight container and store in a cool, dry place.

Before using, stir the mix to redistribute ingredients evenly, as settling may occur. Use as directed in the recipes that follow.

Orange Coconut Cookies

Mix ⅔ C. butter-flavored shortening, 1 egg, 1 tsp. each vanilla and orange extract, ¼ C. orange marmalade, and **3 C. Cookie Mix** on low speed until dough comes together. Stir in 1 C. shredded coconut. Shape into 1" balls and roll in more coconut. Bake on prepped cookie sheets as indicated, until lightly browned. *Makes 2½ dozen*

 375°   8-11 min.

Double Chocolate Mint Buttons

Cut ½ C. shortening into **1¾ C. Cookie Mix** until crumbly. Beat in 1 egg, ½ C. unsweetened cocoa powder, 1 tsp. mint extract, and 1 T. water on low speed until dough forms. Stir in ½ C. mini chocolate chips. Roll into 1" balls and bake on prepped cookie sheets as indicated. Frost with **Chocolate Buttercream** *(page 60). Makes 2½ dozen*

 375°    7-9 min.

Chocolate Chippers

½ C. shortening*
2½ C. Cookie Mix
1 egg
2 tsp. vanilla

1 tsp. water, if needed
¾ C. chocolate chips
(any flavor)

** Use plain or butter-flavored shortening, or use ¼ C. each
shortening and butter (softened).*

Cut shortening into **Cookie Mix** until fine crumbs form. Beat in
egg and vanilla on low speed for 1 minute until dough holds
together, adding water as needed. Stir in chocolate chips. Drop
dough by tablespoonful onto prepped cookie sheets and bake
as indicated, until lightly browned. *Makes 2½ dozen*

18

 350° 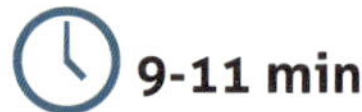 9-11 min.

Candy Bar Blitz

½ C. butter
¼ C. light corn syrup
¾ C. chunky peanut butter, divided

2 C. Cookie Mix

½ C. quick oats
2 C. semi-sweet chocolate chips
1 C. butterscotch chips
1 C. dry roasted peanuts

In a big saucepan over low heat, stir butter, corn syrup, and ¼ cup peanut butter until melted. Stir in **Cookie Mix** and oats. Press mixture into a well-greased 9 x 13″ pan and bake as indicated, until lightly browned. Cool completely.

Microwave both chips with remaining ½ cup peanut butter for 1 to 2 minutes, stirring until melted; stir in peanuts. Spread over cookie base and chill until set; cut into bars. *Serves 24-32*

 375° 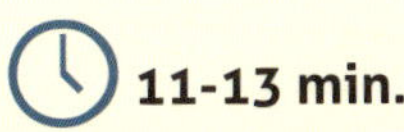 11-13 min.

19

Cut-Out Sugar Cookies

½ C. butter, softened
3 C. Cookie Mix
1 egg

1½ tsp. vanilla
2 T. half & half or
heavy cream

Cut butter into **Cookie Mix** until fine crumbs form. Beat in egg, vanilla, and half & half on low speed until dough comes together. Cover and chill 2 hours *(or overnight)*.

To bake, roll out dough on a floured surface until ¼" thick. Cut with cookie cutters, rerolling scraps. Bake on prepped cookie sheets as indicated. Frost as desired when cool *(recipes on pages 60-61)*. *Makes 3 dozen*

 375°  6-9 min.

Oreo Cheesecake Bars

1 batch prepared sugar cookie dough *(recipe on page 20)*

1 (14.3 oz.) pkg. Oreo cookies

2 (8 oz.) pkgs. cream cheese, softened

½ C. sugar

2 eggs

½ tsp. vanilla

Pinch of salt

Press prepped dough into a parchment paper-lined 9 x 13" pan. Top with a single layer of Oreos. In a bowl, beat cream cheese with sugar until creamy; beat in remaining ingredients and pour over cookie layer. Crush remaining Oreos and sprinkle on top. Bake as indicated, until center is set and only slightly jiggly. Chill at least 2 hours. Remove bars from pan and slice. *Serves 24*

 325° 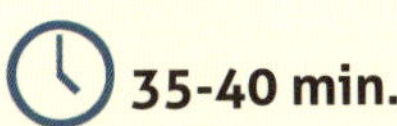 35-40 min.

Snickerdoodles

Combine **3 C. Cookie Mix** and 2 tsp. cream of tartar. Cut in 1 C. softened butter until fine crumbs form. Add 2 eggs and 2 tsp. vanilla; beat on high speed until light, 1 to 2 minutes. Chill dough in the freezer for 30 minutes; shape into 1" balls and roll in cinnamon-sugar. Bake on prepped cookie sheets as indicated. *Makes 3½ dozen*

 375°    7-10 min.

Monster Bars

Mix ½ C. shortening with ¼ C. peanut butter; cut in **2 C. Cookie Mix** and ¾ C. quick oats until crumbly. Stir in 1 egg and 1 tsp. vanilla until mixed, then stir in ¾ C. M&Ms and ½ C. each chocolate chips and chopped pecans. Press into a prepped 9 x 13" pan and bake as indicated, until lightly browned. Cool before cutting. *Serves 18*

 350°    20-24 min.

Cranberry–Cashew Bars

Cut ½ C. softened butter into **1½ C. Cookie Mix** until crumbly. Beat in 2 T. maple syrup, 1 egg, and 1 tsp. vanilla until creamy, 1 to 2 minutes. Stir in ½ C. each old-fashioned oats, chopped cashews, and dried cranberries. Spread in a well-greased 9 x 9" pan and sprinkle with ½ C. white baking chips. Bake as indicated. Cut when cool. *Serves 16*

 350°  18-22 min.

Carrot Spice Cookies

Cut ½ C. softened butter into **2½ C. Cookie Mix** until crumbly. On low speed, beat in 1 egg and ¾ tsp allspice until dough forms. Stir in ½ C. each finely grated carrot, chopped raisins, and chopped walnuts. Drop by spoonful onto prepped cookie sheets and bake as indicated. Frost with **Cream Cheese Frosting** (*page 60*).
Makes 2½ dozen

 375° 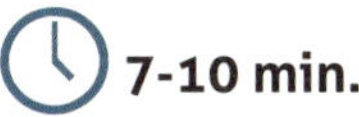 7-10 min.

Peanut Butter Cup Cookies

⅓ C. butter, softened
¼ C. creamy peanut butter
2½ C. Cookie Mix
1 egg

1 tsp. vanilla
Sugar
36 to 42 mini peanut
   butter cups

 375° 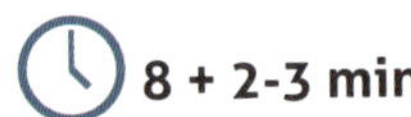 8 + 2-3 min.

In a mixing bowl, beat together the butter and peanut butter until light and creamy. Add **Cookie Mix** and beat until crumbly. Add egg and vanilla, mixing on low speed about 2 minutes, until dough just comes together. Roll dough into generous 1" balls and coat in sugar. Place balls in well-greased mini muffin tins *(do not use paper liners)*. Bake for 8 minutes as indicated.

Remove pan from oven and press a peanut butter cup into the center of each cookie until surrounded by dough. Return to oven to bake 2 to 3 minutes longer. *Makes 3 to 3½ dozen*

Star Power

Turn this same cookie dough into everyone's favorite, *Peanut Butter Star Cookies*. Arrange sugared dough balls on prepped cookie sheets and bake 8 to 9 minutes as directed. Press a chocolate star into each cookie and return to the oven for another minute or two. Beautiful!

Cake Master Mix

13⅓ C. all-purpose flour

8 C. sugar

6 T. baking powder

1½ T. salt

Combine all ingredients in a very large bowl and mix with a wire whisk until evenly combined. Transfer to a labeled airtight container and store in a cool dry place.

Before using, stir the mix to redistribute ingredients evenly, as settling may occur. Use as directed in the recipes that follow.

(3⅓ C. Cake Master Mix equals 1 (15.25 to 16.5 oz.) package yellow cake mix. For a 9 x 13" pan, beat in 1 C. milk, ½ C. oil, 3 eggs, and 1 tsp. vanilla.)

Shelf life 3-4 months

Yellow Cake

Cut ¾ C. shortening into **4 C. Cake Mix** until crumbly. Beat in 3 eggs, 1 C. milk, and 1 tsp. clear vanilla on low speed until blended, then beat 2 minutes more on medium. Spread in prepped pans and bake; frost when cool (try **Baker's Frosting**, page 61). *Makes 2 (8") layers*

White Cake: Substitute 3 ¾ C. **Cake Mix** and 3 lightly beaten egg whites. Mix in other ingredients above and bake.

 350°  25-35 min.

Chocolate Cake

Mix **3 C. Cake Mix** and ¾ C. unsweetened cocoa powder; cut in ¾ C. butter or shortening until crumbly. Beat in 3 eggs, 1 C. milk, and 1 tsp. vanilla until blended, then beat 2 minutes more on medium. Stir in 2 oz. melted semi-sweet baking chocolate. Spread in a prepped pan and bake as indicated. Frost when cool (try **Sour Cream Chocolate Frosting**, page 60). *Makes 1 (9 x 13") cake*

 350° 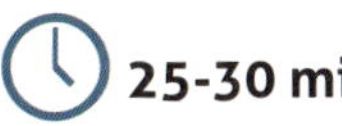 25-30 min.

Spice Cake

4 C. Cake Mix

1 tsp. cinnamon
½ tsp. nutmeg
⅛ tsp. each cloves & allspice
¼ C. butter, softened

½ C. vegetable oil
3 eggs
1 C. milk
2 tsp. vanilla

Whisk together **Cake Mix** and all spices. Cut in butter until crumbly. Add oil, eggs, milk, and vanilla and beat on low speed for 1 minute. Beat on medium for 2 minutes more, until smooth. Pour batter into prepped pans and bake as indicated. Remove from pans after 10 minutes and cool completely before frosting (*try* **Cream Cheese Frosting** *on page 60*). *Makes 2 (8") layers*

 350°

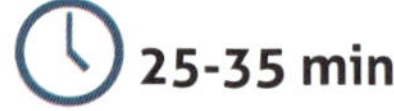 25-35 min.

Berry Bundt Cake

⅔ C. vegetable oil

⅔ C. milk

3½ C. Cake Mix

3 eggs

1 (3 oz.) pkg. strawberry or raspberry gelatin

Combine all ingredients and beat on low speed for 1 minute. Scrape bowl and beat on medium for 1 minute more, until smooth. Pour batter into a prepped Bundt pan and bake as indicated. Cool for 10 minutes before inverting onto a platter; cool completely. Top with whipped cream and fresh berries.

Makes 1 (10") Bundt cake

 350°

 35-40 min.

Pumpkin Chiffon Cake

5 eggs, separated
½ C. vegetable oil
1¼ C. pumpkin puree
1 tsp. cinnamon
½ tsp. each ginger & nutmeg

¼ tsp. cloves
3½ C. Cake Mix
½ tsp. cream of tartar
¼ C. sugar

 325°
 55-65 min.

In a large mixing bowl, combine 5 egg yolks, oil, pumpkin, and all spices; mix on low speed until smooth, about 1 minute. Add **Cake Mix** and beat on high about 1 minute; set aside.

In a separate bowl, beat together 5 egg whites, cream of tartar, and sugar on high speed until glossy firm peaks form *(not dry)*. Fold ¼ of the egg white mixture into batter; then gently fold in remainder until blended. Line the bottom of an ungreased angel food cake pan with parchment paper; pour batter into pan and bake as indicated.

Invert pan onto a bottle to cool completely. Run a thin knife around edge and center of pan to remove cake. Drizzle with **Simple Glaze** *(page 61)* or sprinkle with powdered sugar before slicing. *Makes 1 (10") tube cake*

Secret to Chiffon

When making chiffon cakes, beat eggs in a clean metal or glass bowl *(not plastic)*. Peaks should stand up and just barely fall back on themselves. Avoid using nonstick baking pans and do not grease them. The batter needs to cling to the side of the pan as it rises and bakes to give the cake a light, moist texture.

Maple Nut Cupcakes

¾ C. butter, softened
3½ C. Cake Mix
2 eggs
¾ C. buttermilk

½ C. pure maple syrup
½ tsp. vanilla
½ tsp. maple flavoring
½ C. chopped walnuts

Cut butter into **Cake Mix**. In another bowl, mix eggs, buttermilk, syrup, vanilla, and maple flavoring. Beat half the egg mixture into cake mixture on low speed for 1 minute; gradually beat in the remainder on high speed; stir in nuts. Spoon into prepped muffin cups and bake as indicated. Frost cooled cupcakes with **Basic Buttercream** (*page 60*), using maple flavoring in place of vanilla. *Makes 2 dozen*

32

 350°

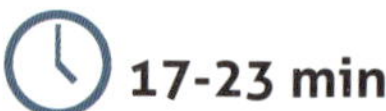 17-23 min.

Lemon Pound Cake

1½ C. butter, softened
3 C. Cake Mix
3 eggs
¾ C. milk

1 tsp. vanilla
1 tsp. lemon extract
1 T. lemon zest

Cut butter into **Cake Mix**. In another bowl, beat eggs with remaining ingredients for 30 seconds. Beat half the egg mixture into cake mixture on high speed for 1 minute. Beat in half of remaining egg mixture, then beat in the remainder. Spread in a prepped loaf pan and bake as indicated. Cool 10 minutes before removing from pan. Drizzle with **Lemon Glaze** (*page 61*).

Makes 1 (5 x 9") loaf cake

 350°  50-60 min.

Cookies & Cream Cuppies

Beat 3 egg whites until foamy. Beat in ⅔ C. vegetable oil, **3¾ C. Cake Mix**, 1 C. milk, and 1 tsp. vanilla on low speed for 1 minute. Add 1 C. crushed Oreo cookies and beat 1½ minutes more. Spoon batter into prepped muffin cups and bake as indicated. Pipe on **Baker's Frosting** *(page 61)* and sprinkle with more crushed cookies. *Makes 2 dozen*

 350°    18-24 min.

Chocolate Bundt

Mix **3¾ C. Cake Mix**, 1 (3.9 oz.) pkg. chocolate instant pudding mix, 3 eggs, ½ C. each water and vegetable oil, 1 C. sour cream, and 1 tsp. vanilla on medium speed for 2 minutes. Bake in a prepped Bundt pan. Cool 10 minutes, then invert onto a platter. Drizzle with **Sour Cream Chocolate Frosting** *(page 60)*; top with cherry pie filling and whipped cream. *Makes 1 (10") Bundt cake*

 350°    40-50 min.

Rhubarb Cake

Combine **3 ¾ C. Cake Mix** and ⅓ C. brown sugar. Cut in ½ C. softened butter until fine crumbs form. Add 2 eggs, 1 C. buttermilk, 1 tsp. vanilla, and ½ tsp. cinnamon; beat on medium speed for 2 minutes, until smooth. Stir in 1½ C. diced rhubarb. Spread in a prepped pan and bake as indicated. Garnish when cool.

Makes 1 (9 x 13") cake

 350°    35-40 min.

Mandarin Cobbler Cake

Mix **4 C. Cake Mix**, 3 eggs, ½ C. vegetable oil, ½ C. sour cream, 2 tsp. orange zest, and 1 tsp. vanilla on low speed until blended. Beat on medium speed for 1 minute more. Stir in 1 (11 oz.) can drained, chopped mandarin oranges. Spread batter in a prepped pan and bake as indicated. Frost with whipped topping.

Makes 1 (9 x 13") cake

 350°   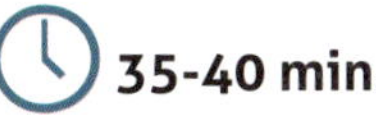 35-40 min.

Pineapple Upside-Down Cake

⅔ C. shortening

4⅓ C. Cake Mix

2 eggs

1 C. milk

1 tsp. vanilla

½ C. butter

⅔ C. light brown sugar

1 (15 oz.) can pineapple slices, drained

12 maraschino cherries, drained

350° 35-40 min.

In a large mixing bowl, cut shortening into **Cake Mix** until crumbly. Add eggs, milk, and vanilla; beat on low speed for 2 minutes, until batter is light and smooth.

For the topping, place butter in a 9 x 13" pan and set in the preheating oven a few minutes to melt; stir in brown sugar and spread evenly. Arrange pineapple slices over butter mixture, halving as needed, and place cherries inside the rings. Spoon batter over the top, spreading evenly. Bake as indicated and let cool 10 minutes before inverting onto a platter to cool completely. *Makes 1 (9 x 13") cake*

Peach Upside-Down Cake

Drain and use 1 (15 oz.) can sliced peaches or frozen *(thawed)* peach slices in place of the pineapple – just fan them out in the pan. For a round cake, use a 12" cast iron skillet instead of a 9 x 13" pan and substitute dark brown sugar; reduce baking time slightly. Serve with whipped cream or ice cream.

This versatile baking mix replaces products such as Bisquick, and one batch is enough to prepare four to eight different recipes.

All-Purpose Master Mix

10 C. all-purpose flour
½ C. baking powder
2 T. sugar
2 tsp. salt

½ tsp. cream of tartar
Scant 1½ C. canola oil
  (or 2 C. shortening)

Mix all dry ingredients in a very large bowl. Gradually beat in oil *(or shortening)* with an electric mixer for 4 to 5 minutes or until texture is fine and even, breaking up any lumps with your hands. Store in an airtight container in a cool, dry place or refrigerate.

Before using, stir the mix to redistribute ingredients evenly, as settling may occur. Use as directed in the recipes that follow.

Shelf life 2-3 months

Fruit Cobbler

Spread 4 C. fruit in a greased 8 x 8" pan *(we used fresh blueberries and canned peaches, drained)*. In a bowl, combine **1 C. All-Purpose Mix** and ¾ C. sugar. Stir in 1 egg until crumbly dough forms. Drop dough evenly over fruit and drizzle with ½ C. melted butter. Bake as indicated. Serve warm or cold. *Serves 6-8*

 350°  38-45 min.

Strawberry Shortcake

Combine 2 to 3 C. sliced fresh strawberries with ¼ C. sugar; let stand. Mix **3 C. All-Purpose Mix** with 2 T. sugar and ¾ C. milk until dough forms. For each shortcake, drop about ⅓ C. dough onto a prepped cookie sheet and bake as indicated; let cool. Split shortcakes in half and top with berries and whipped topping. *Serves 8*

 450°  9-12 min.

Baking Powder Biscuits

3 C. All-Purpose Mix   2 T. butter, melted
¾ to 1 C. milk *(or buttermilk)*

Combine **All-Purpose Mix** with enough milk to make a soft dough. For rolled biscuits *(shown above)*, knead dough 10 times on a surface sprinkled generously with some of the dry mix or flour. Pat dough lightly to ½" thickness and cut rounds with a 2½" cutter; place on a prepped cookie sheet. For drop biscuits, simply drop large spoonfuls of dough onto a prepped or ungreased cookie sheet.

Bake as indicated, then brush butter over warm biscuits.
Makes 8-10 biscuits

 450°    7-11 min.

Cheesy Herbed Biscuits

3 C. All-Purpose Mix

⅓ C. shredded cheddar cheese

½ tsp. garlic powder

¾ to 1 C. milk *(or buttermilk)*

1 tsp. minced fresh parsley or oregano

2 T. butter, melted

Stir together **All-Purpose Mix**, cheese, and garlic powder. Then stir in enough milk to make a soft dough. Drop dough by large spoonful onto a prepped cookie sheet and bake as indicated.

Stir parsley into the butter and brush mixture over hot biscuits. *(Try other cheese, spice, and herb combos, too. Delish!)*

Makes 8-10 biscuits

 450° 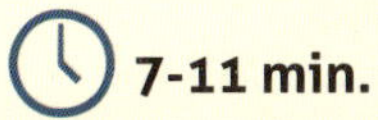 7-11 min.

Blueberry Pancakes

Whisk together 1 C. buttermilk *(or milk)* and 2 eggs. Add **2 C. All-Purpose Mix** and stir until blended. Fold in ¾ C. fresh blueberries. For each pancake, pour ¼ C. batter onto a hot greased griddle and cook until edges are slightly dry. Flip and cook until golden brown. Serve hot with butter and syrup.

Makes 12 pancakes

 Med.  2-4 min.

Waffle Perfection

Beat 1 egg white until glossy stiff peaks form. In another bowl, whisk together **2 C. All-Purpose Mix**, 1⅓ C. milk, 2 T. melted butter, and 1 egg yolk until smooth. Fold in egg white until blended. Pour batter into a greased and heated waffle iron and cook according to manufacturer's directions, until golden brown. Serve hot with butter and syrup.

Serves 4

 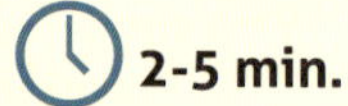 2-5 min.

Beer Bread

Whisk together **3 C. All-Purpose Mix**, ⅓ C. sugar, and 12 oz. beer *(or lemon-lime soda)* until well blended. Pour into a loaf pan with a greased bottom and bake as indicated, until bread tests done. Brush 2 T. melted butter over hot loaf and return to oven for 3 to 5 minutes. Cool at least 15 minutes before slicing.
Makes 1 (5 x 9") loaf

 350°    42-50 min.

Soft Dumplings

Stir together **1 C. All-Purpose Mix** and ¼ C. milk until dough forms. Tear off 1" pieces or drop dough by spoonful into boiling soup or stew. Reduce heat and cover pot; simmer for 15 to 20 minutes, until dumplings are no longer doughy.
Serves 6-8

 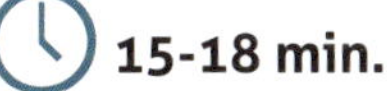 Med-Low   15-18 min.

Apple Fritters

2 C. All-Purpose Mix

⅓ C. sugar

½ tsp. each salt & cinnamon

¼ tsp. nutmeg

2 tart apples, peeled
& chopped

¾ C. apple cider

2 eggs, lightly beaten

2 T. butter, melted

Vegetable oil for frying

Cinnamon-Sugar *(recipe
on page 62)*

Combine **All-Purpose Mix**, sugar, salt, and spices; stir in apples. In another bowl, mix cider, eggs, and butter; add to apple mixture and stir well. Drop batter by heaping tablespoonful into 2" of hot oil and fry about 2 minutes per side, until deep golden brown. Drain on paper towels and sprinkle with **Cinnamon-Sugar**. Serve promptly. *Makes 2½ dozen*

 350°  3-5 min.

Easy Ham & Bacon Quiche

1 C. finely chopped ham

1 C. shredded Swiss or
   cheddar cheese

1½ C. milk

3 eggs

⅓ C. All-Purpose Mix

1 tsp. dried minced onion

Salt & black pepper to taste

Cooked, crumbled bacon

Chopped fresh herbs,
   optional

Layer ham and cheese in a greased 9" pie plate. Mix next four ingredients in a blender on medium speed about 1 minute. Pour egg mixture over meat and cheese and season with salt and pepper. Bake as indicated, until set and a toothpick inserted in the center comes out clean. Sprinkle with bacon and herbs, if you'd like. Serve warm or cold. *Serves 6*

 325° 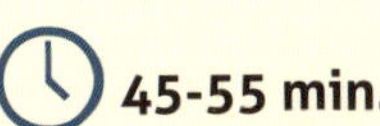 45-55 min.

45

Honey-Kissed Scones

2 eggs
2 T. honey
½ C. heavy cream
  (or half & half)
3½ C. All-Purpose Mix

Optional add-ins: orange zest plus dried cranberries softened in hot water; mini chocolate chips; lemon zest plus fresh blueberries

Whisk together eggs, honey, and cream. Stir in **All-Purpose Mix** until just blended. Gently stir in any add-ins you like *(drained & patted dry)*. Pat ⅓ of the dough at a time into a ½"-thick circle on a floured surface and cut into six wedges. Bake on prepped cookie sheets as indicated, until golden brown. Serve warm, with or without a glaze *(page 61)*. *Makes 18 scones*

46

 400° 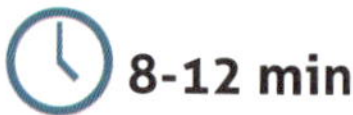 8-12 min.

Biscuit Cinna-Rolls

4½ C. All-Purpose Mix
1⅓ C. milk
3 T. butter, softened

⅓ to ½ C. brown sugar
2 tsp. cinnamon

Stir together **All-Purpose Mix** and milk until just blended. On a floured surface, knead dough 10 times and then roll out into a 12 x 18" rectangle. Spread with butter and sprinkle with brown sugar and cinnamon. Starting at one long side, roll dough into a log, sealing the edge. Cut into 1½"-thick slices and place in greased muffin cups; bake as indicated. Drizzle with **Simple Glaze** *(page 61). Makes 1 dozen*

 400°   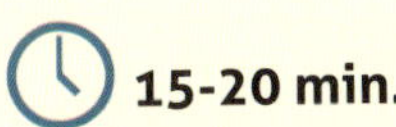 15-20 min.

Yeast Bread Master Mix

6 C. all-purpose flour
6 C. bread flour
8 tsp. instant/rapid-rise yeast

¼ C. sugar
3 tsp. salt

Combine all ingredients in a very large bowl and whisk until evenly combined. Transfer to a labeled airtight container and store in the refrigerator for best results. *(Cut the recipe in half if your fridge space is limited.)*

Before using, stir the mix to redistribute ingredients evenly, as settling may occur. Use as directed in the recipes that follow.

Refrigerate 2-3 months

Homebaked Bread

Heat ¾ C. water, ¼ C. milk, and 1 T. butter until very warm *(120° to 130°)*. Put **2¾ C. Bread Mix** into a stand mixing bowl. Gradually beat in warm milk mixture on medium speed for 2 minutes. Increase speed and beat just until dough is elastic and pulls cleanly away from bowl. Knead on a floured surface for 2 minutes, until smooth and no longer sticky. Cover and let rest 10 minutes.

Flatten dough, pressing out big air bubbles, and shape as desired. For a **loaf**, roll into a log and tuck ends underneath. Place seam side down in a greased 5 x 9" loaf pan. For **dinner rolls**, cut dough into 12 or 15 equal pieces and shape into balls. Set smooth side up in a greased 9 x 13" pan. Cover and let rise in a warm place until doubled in size, 50 to 60 minutes. Bake as indicated. *Makes 1 loaf or 12-15 dinner rolls*

 375°  **40-45 min.** *(loaf)* **15-20 min.** *(rolls)*

Herbed Focaccia

In a stand mixing bowl, combine **2¾ C. Bread Mix**, 1 tsp. each garlic powder and dried oregano, ½ tsp. dried basil, and ⅛ tsp. black pepper. Heat 1 C. water to 120° to 130°; add 2 T. olive oil and pour water mixture gradually into bowl, beating on medium speed about 2½ minutes, until dough is elastic. Knead on a floured surface for 2 minutes, until smooth. Divide dough among two greased 8 x 8″ pans and press flat. Cover and let rest in a warm place for 20 to 30 minutes *(it will rise slightly)*.

Press finger indentations in dough about ½″ apart. Brush with oil, then sprinkle with ½ tsp. coarse salt and Parmesan cheese. Bake as indicated, until golden brown. Cut and serve, or slice and use for sandwiches *(we used grilled chicken, mozzarella, tomato, lettuce, and onion)*. *Serves 8*

 425°

 14-18 min.

Soft & Chewy Pretzels

Combine **4 C. Bread Mix**, 5 T. brown sugar, and 5 tsp. baking powder in a stand mixing bowl. Beat in 1¼ C. very warm water *(120° to 130°)* on low speed for 2 to 3 minutes, until dough forms. Knead on a floured surface for 2 minutes, then form a ball. Turn dough in an oiled bowl, cover, and let rise in a warm place for 1 hour. Divide dough in half. Flatten each half into a long rectangle and cut each into 12 strips. Roll the strips into 24 thin ropes, 20" to 22" long, then bend into pretzel shapes.

Simmer 4 C. water in a saucepan; slowly stir in ⅓ C. baking soda. Gently set each pretzel in soda bath for a few seconds; remove to prepped cookie sheets and sprinkle with coarse salt. Bake as indicated, until deep golden brown. Brush with melted butter and serve warm. *Makes 2 dozen*

 425°　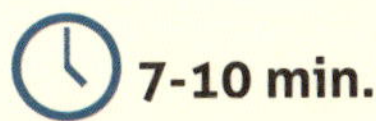 7-10 min.

Pizza Crust

Measure **3 C. Bread Mix** into a bowl. Heat 1 C. plus 2 T. water until very warm *(120° to 130°)*. Add 2 T. vegetable oil and immediately stir water mixture into bowl until a sticky dough forms, about 1 minute. Cover and let rest 15 minutes.

Press dough into a greased 14" pizza pan *(or divide dough among two smaller pans for thinner crusts)*. Let rest at least 5 minutes while oven preheats to 500°. Prebake crust for 3 to 5 minutes, until set.

Reduce oven temperature to 400°. Spread prebaked crust with sauce and toppings you like. Bake as indicated on the lowest oven rack until crust is lightly browned and cheese is melted. *Makes 1 (14") pizza*

 400°

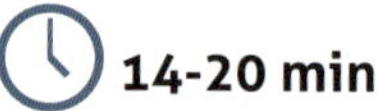 14-20 min.

Calzones

Heat ⅔ C. water to 120° to 130°; add 1 T. vegetable oil and immediately stir water mixture into **2 C. Bread Mix** until a sticky dough forms. Knead on a floured surface for 5 minutes, until smooth and elastic. Cover and let rest 15 to 30 minutes.

Cut dough into four even pieces and flatten each into an 8" circle on a floured surface. Spread desired fillings on half the circle, leaving ¾" of edge uncovered *(we used ½ C. buffalo chicken and ¼ C. shredded mozzarella for each)*. Fold other half of dough over filling and press edges together; fold edge back and press again with your knuckle to seal. Set on a prepped cookie sheet and brush with oil. Sprinkle with coarse salt and cut steam vents in tops. Bake as indicated, until golden brown. Serve with your favorite sauce. *Makes 4 calzones*

 425° 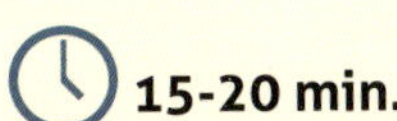 15-20 min.

Cinnamon Swirl Raisin Bread

Place **2⅔ C. Bread Mix** in a stand mixing bowl and beat in
1 C. very warm water *(120° to 130°)* on low speed for 3 minutes,
until a sticky dough forms; cover mixer with a towel and let rest
7 minutes. Beat on low speed for 3 minutes more, until smooth
but still tacky. Turn dough out onto a floured surface and knead
5 times. Sprinkle dough with 3 T. **Cinnamon-Sugar** *(page 62)* and
½ C. golden raisins and work both into dough until combined.
Shape dough into a free-form loaf, tucking ends underneath and
pinching seams. Place on a prepped cookie sheet, cover, and let
rise in a warm place about 45 minutes.

Let dough rest while oven preheats. Just before baking, slash
top of loaf several times with a sharp knife. Bake as indicated,
until deep golden brown. *Makes 1 loaf*

54

400°

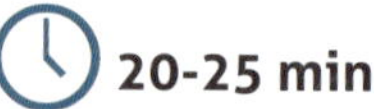

20-25 min.

Fluffy Garlic Breadsticks

Put **2¾ C. Bread Mix** into a stand mixing bowl. Heat 1 C. water and 3 T. butter until very warm *(120° to 130°)*; gradually add to bread mix and beat on medium speed for 2 minutes. Beat on high briefly, until dough is elastic and pulls cleanly away from bowl. Knead on a floured surface for 2 minutes, until smooth. Cover and let rest 10 minutes.

Roll dough into a 9 x 12" rectangle, pushing out air bubbles. Cut 12 crosswise strips, then cut in half lengthwise. Roll and twist strips into breadsticks, 6" to 7" long. *(Or, for "pull-aparts," simply set strips ½" apart on prepped cookie sheets.)* Cover and let rise in a warm place 50 to 60 minutes and bake as indicated. Brush with a mixture of 3 T. melted butter, ½ tsp. sea salt, and ¼ tsp. each garlic powder and Italian seasoning. *Makes 2 dozen*

 400° 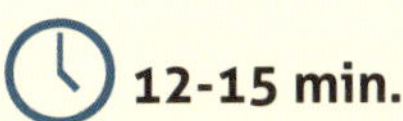 12-15 min.

Brownie Master Mix

6 C. all-purpose flour

8 C. sugar

2⅔ C. unsweetened cocoa
  powder

4 tsp. baking powder

4 tsp. salt

Whisk together all ingredients in a large bowl and work with your hands to break up any lumps. Transfer to a labeled airtight container and store in a cool, dry place.

Before using, stir the mix to redistribute ingredients evenly as settling may occur. Use as directed in the recipes that follow.

(3 C. Brownie Master Mix equals 1 (18.3 oz.) package. To prep a 9 x 13" pan, add ¼ C. water, ⅔ C. oil, 1 tsp. vanilla, and 2 or 3 eggs.)

Shelf life 2-3 months

Fudge Brownies

Stir together **2¼ C. Brownie Mix**, 2 eggs, ¼ C. melted butter, 1 tsp. vanilla, and 1 tsp. water until smooth. Add ½ C. optional stir-ins *(try chopped nuts, baking chips, or crushed Oreos).* Spread in a prepped 8 x 8" or 9 x 9" pan and bake as indicated, until edges begin to pull away. When cool, frost with **Chocolate Buttercream** *(page 60).*

Makes 1 square pan

 350°    22-30 min.

S'mores Brownies

Mix **3½ C. Brownie Mix**, 3 eggs, ⅔ C. vegetable oil, 2 tsp. vanilla, and 2 T. water with a spoon until smooth. Spread in a greased 9 x 13" pan and bake as indicated. Sprinkle warm brownies with 2 C. mini marshmallows and 1 C. each milk chocolate chips and broken graham crackers. Let cool.

Makes 1 (9 x 13") pan

 350°    25-32 min.

Peanut Butter Cheesecake Brownies

3 C. Brownie Mix

¼ C. water

⅔ C. vegetable oil

2 eggs

1 tsp. vanilla

1 (8 oz.) pkg. cream cheese, softened

¾ C. creamy peanut butter

½ C. sugar

1 egg

1 T. flour

½ tsp. vanilla

Mix first five ingredients until smooth. In another bowl, beat cream cheese on medium speed until creamy, then beat in next five ingredients. Spread most of brownie batter in a well greased 9 x 13" pan. Spoon cream cheese mixture and rest of brownie batter on top; swirl with a knife. Bake as indicated and let cool. (Try **Peanut Butter Frosting** on page 61.) *Makes 1 (9 x 13") pan*

 350°

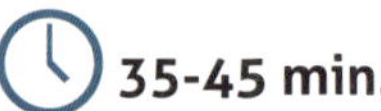 35-45 min.

Brownie Sundae Cake

3 C. Brownie Mix
3 eggs
⅔ C. vegetable oil
1 tsp. vanilla
¼ C. water

½ C. butterscotch chips, divided
½ C. chopped salted caramel almonds, divided
5 C. salted caramel frozen yogurt, softened

Mix first five ingredients until smooth; split among two 9" round pans lined with greased foil. Sprinkle half the chips and almonds over each. Bake as indicated and cool completely. Lift foil to remove brownies. Set one brownie in a 9" springform pan; spread with yogurt. Lightly press second brownie on top, nut side up; cover and freeze overnight. Remove from pan, slice, and garnish. *Serves 12*

 350°   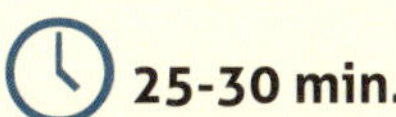 25-30 min.

59

Finishing Touches

Frostings & Glazes *Creamy frostings can be made ahead of time and stored in the refrigerator for up to 1 month in a zippered plastic or piping bag. It's ready anytime you need it – just let warm up slightly before using. Make glazes just before using.*

Basic Buttercream

Beat together ½ C. softened butter, 3¾ C. sifted powdered sugar, pinch of salt, 3 T. milk, and 2 tsp. flavoring on medium speed until creamy. Add food coloring if desired. Spread or pipe on. *(For **Chocolate Buttercream**, add 6 T. sifted unsweetened cocoa powder and 2 tsp. more milk.)*

Sour Cream Chocolate Frosting

Melt 1 C. semi-sweet chocolate chips and ¼ C. butter in a saucepan, stirring until smooth; cool 5 minutes. Transfer to a bowl and beat in ½ C. sour cream, ½ tsp. vanilla, and 2¼ to 2½ C. sifted powdered sugar until smooth and spreadable. *(To drizzle, warm up slightly.)* Refrigerate leftovers.

Cream Cheese Frosting

Beat together 4 oz. softened cream cheese, ¼ C. softened butter, and 2 tsp. vanilla on high speed until smooth. Slowly beat in 2 C. sifted powdered sugar until blended, then beat on high speed 1 to 2 minutes, until light and spreadable.

Baker's Frosting

In a large mixing bowl, combine ¼ C. warm water, ½ C. shortening, ¼ tsp. salt, 1 tsp. clear vanilla, and 4 C. powdered sugar. Beat on low to blend, then beat on high for 10 minutes. Add food coloring as desired. Spread or pipe on.

Peanut Butter Frosting

Beat together ¼ C. softened butter, ¼ C. creamy peanut butter, 1 C. sifted powdered sugar, and 1 T. milk on medium speed until smooth, fluffy, and spreadable.

Simple Glaze

Whisk together 3 T. milk, 1 tsp. clear vanilla, and about 2 C. sifted powdered sugar until smooth. Thicken with more powdered sugar or thin with more milk as needed for drizzling.

Orange Glaze

In a small bowl, whisk together 2 T. orange juice, 1 tsp. orange zest *(optional)*, and enough sifted powdered sugar to make a glaze you like. *(For **Lemon Glaze**, substitute lemon juice and lemon zest.)*

Muffin Toppings Make these toppings ahead of time and refrigerate in airtight containers for up to 3 months. Each topping recipe makes enough for approximately 24 muffins or 2 loaves of quick bread.

Nutty Streusel

In a bowl, combine ⅔ C. flour, ⅔ C. finely chopped nuts *(pecans or walnuts)*, ⅔ C. brown sugar, ½ C. quick oats, and ½ tsp. cinnamon. Add ½ C. melted butter and stir well, until mixture is crumbly.

Zested Sugar

In a bowl, toss 1 to 2 tsp. lemon or orange zest with 2 T. coarse or regular granulated sugar until zest is coated *(choose the citrus flavor that goes best with your recipe)*. Let stand at least 10 minutes before using.

Cinnamon-Sugar

Combine ½ C. sugar and 2 tsp. cinnamon in a zippered plastic bag; shake until well mixed and store in an airtight container. *(This needs no refrigeration.)*

Substitution Tips

Using Whole Wheat Flour

You can successfully substitute whole wheat flour for 25% of the total amount of all-purpose flour listed in these master mix recipes: Muffin, Cookie, All-Purpose, and Yeast Bread. Then simply use the master mixes as directed. For cake and brownie recipes, "plain" cookie recipes *(like cut-out sugar cookies)*, or anything that needs a light airy texture, it's best to stick with all-purpose flour.

Store master mixes containing whole wheat flour in the refrigerator or freezer to maintain freshness. Just warm the mix to room temperature before using.

Going Gluten-Free

Substituting gluten-free flour for all-purpose flour in the master mixes is easy, but following these guidelines will give you the tastiest baked products.

1. Go gluten-free with any of the mixes except the Yeast Bread Master Mix.

2. Choose a "1 to 1" gluten-free baking flour that includes xanthan gum for the simplest swap – just substitute one cup of this flour for each cup of all-purpose flour in the master mix recipe.

3. Some gluten-free baked items have a slightly different, drier texture than those made with all-purpose flour. If a batter or dough seems too thick, add more moisture with a bit of water, slightly more butter, shortening, or oil, and/or an extra egg.

4. Let gluten-free batters or doughs rest for 20 minutes before baking to help reduce any grittiness caused by the flour's ingredients. Add stir-ins after the rest period. *(Cookie dough should rest at least an hour or be refrigerated overnight.)*

5. When a batter or dough has plenty of liquid, like pancakes, waffles, muffins, and quick breads, the finished products are exceptional!